Magda Garguláková and Jakub Bachorík

BRIDGES

post wave

DEAR READER.

A bridge is often the start of a great adventure, and no two bridges are the same. Large ones, small ones, old and modern ones, ordinary and world-changing ones – they all can take us on a journey to another place. So step up, cross the bridge, read on, and discover more.

WHAT ARE BRIDGES?

RECORD HOLDERS

HISTORY

BUILDING A BRIDGE

BRIDGES & CULTURE

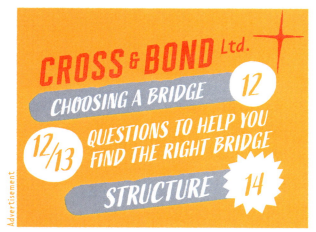
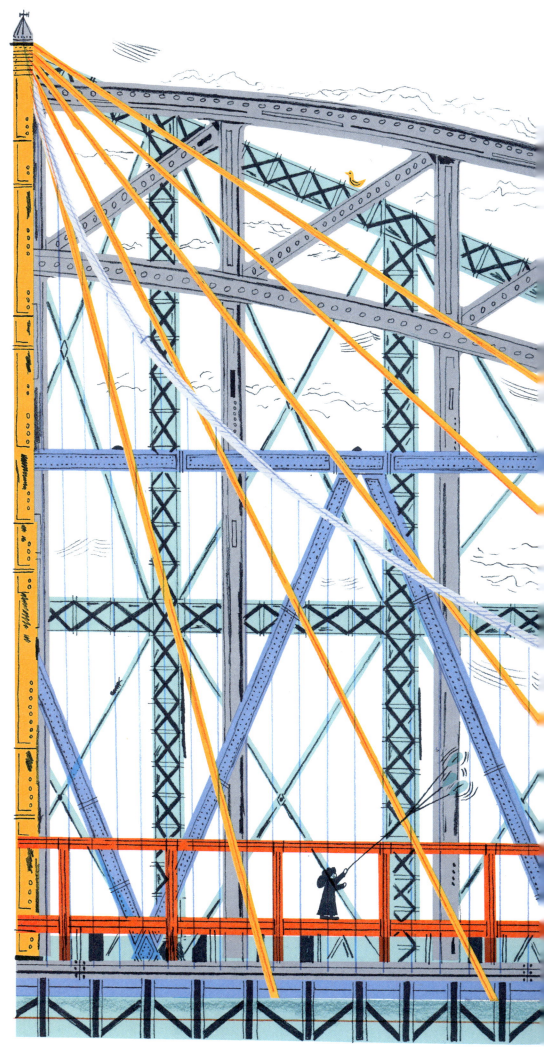

There are so many
obstacles to cross...

What's the solution ?

connecting places

making a safe path

providing security

overcoming obstacles

6

shortening distances

How
BRIDGES
can help us...

adding to the scenery

giving us another point of view

DIFFERENT TYPES OF BRIDGES

movable folding bridge

natural bridge

armored vehicle-launched bridge

observation bridge

suspended footbridge

lifting bridge

pontoon bridge

covered bridge

transporter bridge

play bridge

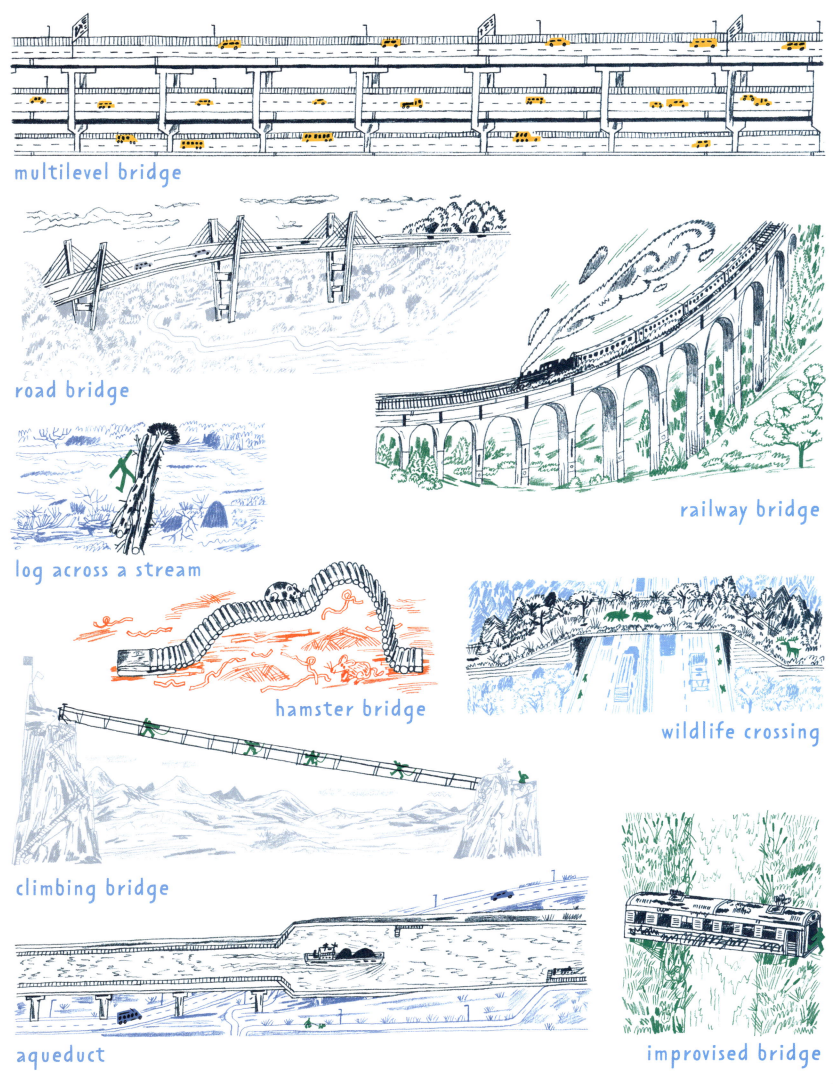

multilevel bridge

road bridge

railway bridge

log across a stream

hamster bridge

wildlife crossing

climbing bridge

aqueduct

improvised bridge

WHAT MAKES A BRIDGE A BRIDGE?

Before we look at different bridges, we need to understand how they work. We learn about the many uses of bridges when we're young, so we've never needed a complicated explanation. But how would you describe a bridge to someone who has never seen one, or to an inhabitant of another planet who has no use for bridges because they fly? Let's start with the basics.

FEATURES OF A BRIDGE

IT CONNECTS PLACES

IT PROVIDES A PATH OVER AN OBSTACLE

IT IS HUMAN-MADE

IT SHORTENS DISTANCES

PARTS OF A BRIDGE

Although some bridges are similar in appearance, each bridge is unique. Yet all have common structural elements that make them a bridge, without which they would lack the stability to take us from one side to the other.

A FOUNDATIONS
Commonly made of concrete, these solid bases anchor the bridge firmly in place on the ground below.

B ABUTMENTS
These support the bridge at its ends and absorb the many forces placed upon it.

C PIERS
Pillars or columns that hold up the bridge and absorb tension bearing down on its structure.

D MAIN SUPPORT STRUCTURE
The horizontal support that carries live traffic, comprising a number of elements.

E DECK
The surface of the bridge where vehicles and people travel, often covered with pavement.

F BEARINGS
Points where the bridge deck connects to the piers. They allow for movement in the structure such as twisting or a back-and-forth motion.

G EXPANSION JOINT AND CLOSURE JOINT
The closure joint overlaps the expansion joint, which is there to allow for any expansion in the support structure, such as from temperature changes.

H FITTINGS
These can include railings, crash barriers, lighting, or water drainage.

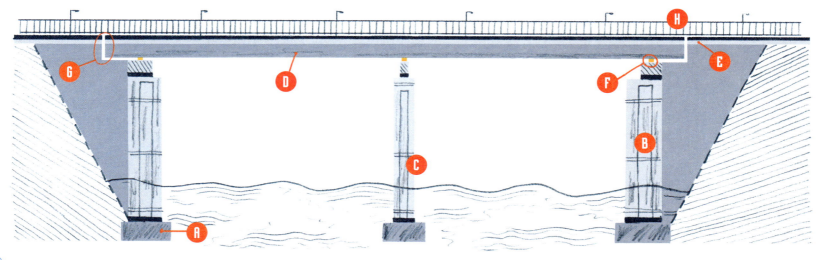

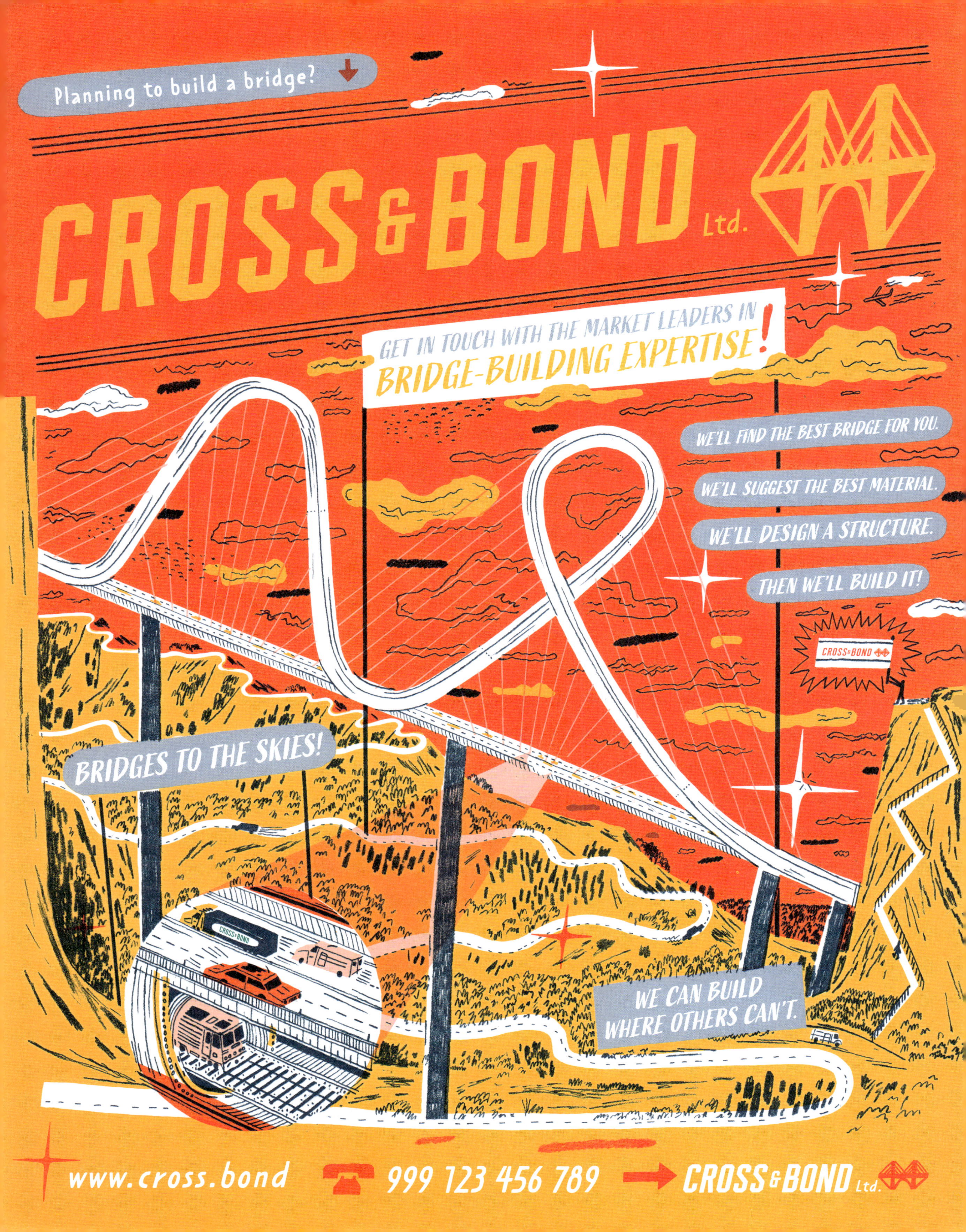

Planning to build a bridge?
CROSS&BOND Ltd.
GET IN TOUCH WITH THE MARKET LEADERS IN
BRIDGE-BUILDING EXPERTISE!
WE'LL FIND THE BEST BRIDGE FOR YOU.
WE'LL SUGGEST THE BEST MATERIAL.
WE'LL DESIGN A STRUCTURE.
THEN WE'LL BUILD IT!
BRIDGES TO THE SKIES!
WE CAN BUILD
WHERE OTHERS CAN'T.
www.cross.bond
999 123 456 789
CROSS&BOND Ltd.

CHOOSING
the Right Bridge

Bridges can be large or small. Some we barely notice; others go down in history. There are hundreds of shapes and styles. A new bridge can transform any village, town, or city. It must be functional, resilient, reliable, and, of course, safe. Choosing the right style and material for a bridge is vital, but will depend on a number of factors, such as what the bridge is for and where it is going.

NO JOB TOO BIG!

STILL IN DOUBT? THEN CONTACT OUR TEAM!

www.cross.bond

HUNDREDS OF SATISFIED CUSTOMERS

When choosing a **BRIDGE**, ask yourself these **QUESTIONS:**

1 What kind of **OBSTACLE** must it overcome?

NATURAL		HUMAN-MADE	NONE
deep valley	wide river	roads, railways	for decoration
narrow stream	jagged fissures	buildings, homes	simply a bridge
impassable terrain		pipelines	

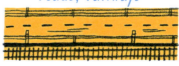

OBSTACLE? WHAT OBSTACLE?

2 WHO or WHAT is the bridge FOR?

WE'LL BRIDGE ANYTHING!

pedestrians

cars

animals

mixed traffic

public transportation

cyclists

water

trains

cables

3 What LENGTH do I need?

5.9 ft

mini bridge
3-6 ft

short-span bridge
6-50 ft

medium-span bridge
50-246 ft

long-span bridge
246-328 ft

mega bridge
328-X* ft

*X = an infinite measurement

4 Which building MATERIAL should I use?

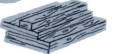

Wood
- cheap, readily available, and easy to process
- short lifespan and low durability
- suitable for small bridges for pedestrians and cyclists

Brick
- cheap, readily available, looks good
- limited lifespan
- suitable for historic structures

Stone
- strong, resilient, reliable
- looks good, can be decorated
- suitable for renovation of historic structures

Steel
- strong, reliable, lightweight
- subject to corrosion
- suitable for long spans

Concrete
- strong, resilient, reliable
- bears heavy loads across long spans
- stronger options: reinforced concrete or prestressed concrete

ordinary concrete

reinforced concrete

prestressed concrete

13

CHOOSING A STRUCTURE

Deciding on the structure is a key moment in bridge-building that requires lots of careful consideration. Each structure type has different characteristics that are suitable for different conditions. Some are more wind-resistant, others are ideal for long distances, while others just look really good. Learning to tell one bridge structure from another isn't always easy or obvious at first glance!

EXAMPLES:

BEAM BRIDGE

DONGHAI

This is the most common, simplest, and oldest bridge structure. The basic deck on a beam bridge is supported at each end by an abutment. It is suitable for bridging shorter distances, although modern materials today allow for greater spans.

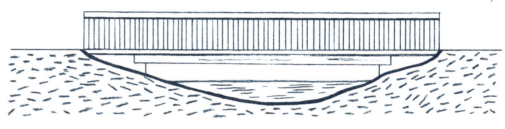

CHEAPEST SOLUTION

TRUSS BRIDGE

QUEBEC

A strong, resilient structure that comes in various shapes and sizes. Truss bridges are made up of interconnected triangles, creating a sturdy framework that can bear heavy loads.

LIGHTWEIGHT STRUCTURE

Mk.*BIXBY*

ARCH BRIDGE

BIXBY & SYDNEY

This widespread, attractive, resilient, and complex structure is made up of one or a succession of arches. Its shape is determined by whether the arch is above, below, or in the middle of the bridge's deck. It is suitable for both short and long bridges.

BEARS A GREAT WEIGHT

DEPENDABLE CLASSIC

Mk.*SYDNEY*

SUSPENSION BRIDGE

GOLDEN GATE

This structure is particularly useful for long distances. The weight of the deck is borne by two main suspension cables, each anchored to a bank by a tower. Steel ropes to hold the deck are lowered from support cables. It is suitable for overcoming wide obstacles and wherever space for support pillars is limited.

CABLE-STAYED BRIDGE

MILLAU

This newest, but most widespread bridge style, has at least one pylon from which the ropes carrying the deck are routed. The arrangement of supporting ropes varies. It is suitable for long and short spans.

DIFFERENT CABLE ARRANGEMENTS

fan

harp

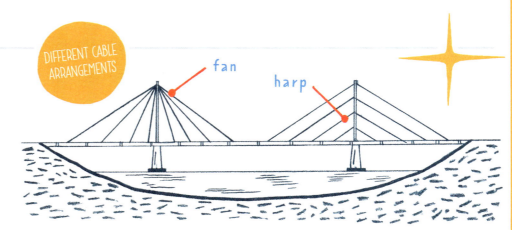

CANTILEVER BRIDGE

FORTH

This is a reliable and simple design that uses a system of beams, called brackets, that project out horizontally across a space. Usually made up of three parts, the two outermost parts are anchored into the bank, which then carry the middle part of the bridge that is 'balanced' between them.

FOR LONG DISTANCES

MOVABLE BRIDGE

GATESHEAD

A useful, widespread, and popular bridge that comes in many types. A part of the bridge, or the whole bridge, is able to move to clear the way for transportation. This bridge is suitable for short and long spans.

NICE TO LOOK AT

swing

bascule

retractable

WIDE RANGE OF OPTIONS

HYBRID BRIDGE

BROOKLYN

Some bridge types can even be combined to meet various needs, such as a hybrid cable-stayed suspension bridge.

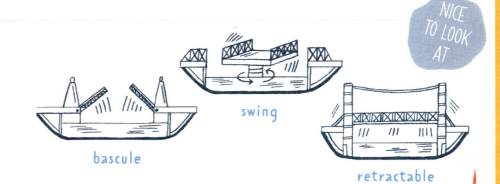

FREE PROFESSIONAL CONSULTATION

office@cross.bond

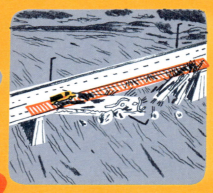

DIFFERENT WORDS FOR A BRIDGE

When we say 'bridge', everyone knows what we mean. But bridges are known by other names too. Look these up in a dictionary and you'll discover quite a few differences. Bridges come in numerous shapes and sizes and have a wide range of uses. Rest assured that if you insist on calling them all a bridge, no one will mind.

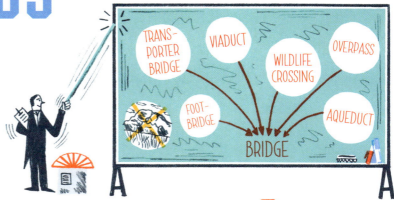

OVERPASS

A bridge over terrain, supported by pillars. Used in places where it would be too complicated to build.

AN OVERPASS LOOKS PRETTY MUCH LIKE A PIER.

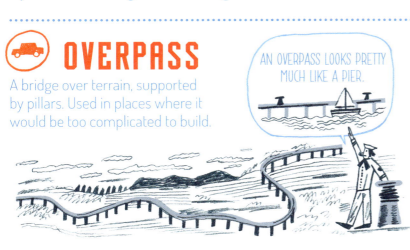

AQUEDUCT

A bridge that carries water.

HOW CLEVER WE ROMANS WERE!

NOW YOU HAVE ONLY PIPES AND SEWERS.

FOOTBRIDGE

A small bridge for pedestrians and/or cyclists. Can also be a lookout point or connect buildings.

VIADUCT

A bridge with a road for pedestrians, cyclists, cars, or trains.

'VIA' IS THE LATIN WORD FOR 'WAY'.

WILDLIFE CROSSING

A bridged path over a busy road or other obstacle for use by wildlife.

TRANSPORTER BRIDGE

A bridge that uses a cage-like suspended ferry to carry passengers, cars, and freight from one bank to the other.

WE ARE AN ENDANGERED SPECIES. THERE ARE ONLY A FEW OF US LEFT.

BUT SOMETIMES A BRIDGE IS SOMETHING ELSE...

Turn to page 62

STATISTICS*

'CITY OF BRIDGES':
Pittsburgh, USA

EASIEST PLACE TO GET LOST ON A BRIDGE:
Venice, Italy

MOST PHOTOGRAPHED BRIDGE:
Golden Gate Bridge, USA

BUSIEST BRIDGE:
George Washington Bridge, New York, USA

LARGEST BRICK BRIDGE:
Göltzsch Viaduct, Germany

NUMBER OF BRIDGES PER CITY: *
St Petersburg 342
Venice 435
Pittsburgh 446
Amsterdam 1,753
New York 2,027
Hamburg 2,428
Chongqing .... over 14,000

NUMBER OF BRIGES PER RIVER: *
Amazon 0
Rhein 102
Vltava 107
Danube 133
Mississippi 142
Yangtze 160
Thames 214

*   Statistics have one drawback: being highly changeable. Consider these as guidance only.

**   Surprisingly hard to calculate. What actually counts as a bridge?

…AND WORLD RECORD BRIDGES?

LONGEST

NAME Danyang-Kunshan Grand Bridge
LENGTH 102 miles
YEAR OPENED 2011

Hartland Bridge

HARTLAND | CANADA

Originally uncovered, the Hartland Bridge spans the Saint John River. In 1922, it was transformed into the world's longest covered bridge, despite initial objections from some locals who believed adding a roof was a bad idea.

LENGTH 1,283 ft
YEAR OPENED 1901

COVERED

LENGTH 1,887 ft **HEIGHT** 253 ft **YEAR** 2013

Pont Jacques Chaban-Delmas

BORDEAUX | FRANCE

This vertical-lift bridge can raise its central section an impressive 197 feet above the water. Despite the lifted section weighing a substantial 2,756 tons, it can be fully elevated in just 11 minutes.

NAME Millau Viaduct **LENGTH** 1.5 miles **HEIGHT** 1,125 ft **YEAR OPENED** 2004

Danyang-Kunshan Grand Bridge

JIANGSU PROVINCE | CHINA

Currently the world's longest bridge at 102 miles, high-speed trains run along the Danyang–Kunshan Grand Bridge between the Chinese cities of Shanghai and Nanjing. But as this record has continually changed throughout history, it could be broken again!

LENGTH 413 ft
HEIGHT 164 ft
YEAR OPENED 2001

MOVABLE

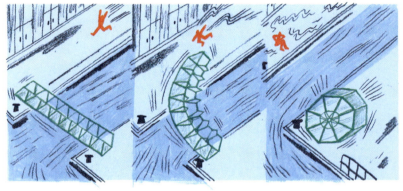

Gateshead Millennium Bridge

GATESHEAD | UNITED KINGDOM

Known as the 'Blinking Eye Bridge' because of its unique tilting design (the first to ever be constructed), the Gateshead Millennium Bridge serves pedestrians and cyclists. When a ship passes underneath, it lifts upward, powered by eight electric engines. This process takes four and a half minutes.

Rolling Bridge

LONDON | UNITED KINGDOM

LENGTH 39 ft
YEAR OPENED 2004

More of an art installation than a functional bridge, this interesting bridge can roll itself up in the manner of an armadillo in only four minutes.

TALLEST

Millau Viaduct

MILLAU | FRANCE

The tallest bridge in Europe is a marvel of modern architecture with a height that adds to, rather than detracts from, its elegance. Designed by French engineer Michel Virlogeux and British architect Norman Foster, the Millau Viaduct has seven pylons of different heights. At its highest point, it is taller than the Eiffel Tower.

Duge Bridge

XUANWEI | CHINA

LENGTH 4,400 ft
HEIGHT 1,854 ft
YEAR OPENED 2016

Currently the world's tallest bridge, the Duge Bridge spans a mountainous valley across the Beipan river at a height of 1,854 feet.

Stari Most

MOSTAR | BOSNIA AND HERZEGOVINA

Built in the 16th century, Stari Most was long the pride and joy of Mostar. It was destroyed during the Croat-Bosniak War in 1993. But the bridge became a symbol of hope when it was rebuilt just a decade later using local stone and the original 16th-century building technology.

LENGTH 95 ft **HEIGHT** 79 ft **YEAR OPENED** 16th century, (rebuilt 2004)

LENGTH 6,016 ft **HEIGHT** 276 ft **YEAR OPENED** 18

Pont du Gard

NÎMES | FRANCE

The world's most famous aqueduct is an eternal mark of ancient Roman ingenuity. Pont du Gard carried an estimated 11,000,000 US gallons of water to the city of Nîmes every day, and was already a tourist attraction in the 18th century.

LENGTH 902 ft
HEIGHT 161 ft
YEAR OPENED 60

FAMOUS

Tower Bridge

LONDON | UNITED KINGDOM

When you think of London, you likely picture Tower Bridge. This distinctive suspension bridge with a lifting center section is a major tourist attraction and city symbol, often featured on souvenirs like tea towels, keyrings, and mugs. Don't confuse it with the London Bridge, which was famously 'falling down'.

LENGTH 800 ft **HEIGHT** 213 ft **YEAR OPENED** 1894

Sydney Harbour Bridge

SYDNEY | AUSTRALIA

A true colossus, with eight lanes of highway, two railway tracks, a cycle track, and pavement for pedestrians, Sydney Harbour Bridge's single arch spans an incredible 1,650 feet.

LENGTH 3,773 ft **HEIGHT** 440 ft **YEAR OPENED** 1932

Ponte di Rialto

VENICE | ITALY

Crossing the Rialto Bridge in Venice is a physical challenge, with everyone vying for a photo from its highest point. It's no surprise that tourists come here, as it offers a stunning view of the Grand Canal.

LENGTH 158 ft **HEIGHT** 25 ft **YEAR OPENED** 1591

Brooklyn Bridge

NEW YORK | USA

A trip to New York would be incomplete without a visit to the Brooklyn Bridge. One of the oldest suspension bridges in North America, and the result of great determination and vision on the part of its builders, it is a key feature of the city's skyline.

LENGTH 394 ft **YEAR OPENED** 1185

Pont Saint-Bénézet

AVIGNON | FRANCE

The bridge that inspired the song '*On the Bridge at Avignon*' is also famous for the fact that it ends in the middle of a river! Since it kept collapsing during floods, the locals decided to stop repairing it – and most of the bridge was destroyed. The four surviving arches of the bridge are now a UNESCO World Heritage Site.

LENGTH 1.6 miles **HEIGHT** 745 ft **YEAR OPENED** 1937

Ponte Vecchio

FLORENCE | ITALY

Much like Florence is filled with art and architecture, this bridge is lined with houses of various shapes and colors. Most host goldsmiths' and jewellers' shops, earning it the nickname 'Goldsmith's Bridge'. Above these shops runs the Vasari Corridor, which connects the town hall to the Palazzo Pitti. The corridor was built for Cosimo de' Medici, the ruler of Florence in the 16th century, who refused to walk among the 'common people'.

LENGTH 312 ft **YEAR OPENED** 1345

Golden Gate Bridge

SAN FRANCISCO | USA

Renowned worldwide, the Golden Gate Bridge is an iconic landmark. Spanning the often turbulent waters of the San Francisco Bay and frequently enveloped in mist, it serves as a captivating subject for photographers, filmmakers, and romantics alike.

Charles Bridge

PRAGUE | CZECH REPUBLIC

Many visit Prague to walk across the Charles Bridge, a centuries-old structure that is expected to endure for many more. According to legend, eggs were mixed into the mortar to strengthen the bridge, but scientists have since debunked this myth.

LENGTH 1,693 ft **HEIGHT** 43 ft **YEAR OPENED** 1402

Alamillo Bridge

SEVILLE | SPAIN

The harp-shaped Alamillo Bridge, embodying lightness, elegance and simplicity, was designed by renowned structural engineer Santiago Calatrava, who has built bridges worldwide.

Rakotzbrücke Devil's Bridge

KROMLAU | GERMANY

Rakotzbrücke Bridge in Germany looks like a setting for a fairy tale or romantic film. This structure, made of dark basalt, was designed so that it creates a perfect circle when reflected in the water below. The bridge was once believed to be built by the Devil due to its unstable arch. Despite this appearance, the bridge is structurally sound, but today visitors are not allowed to walk on it.

LENGTH 115 ft YEAR OPENED 1860

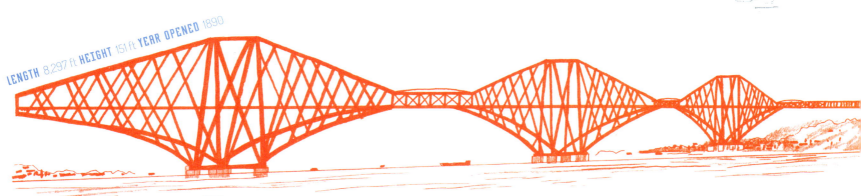

LENGTH 8,297 ft HEIGHT 151 ft YEAR OPENED 1890

Forth Bridge

EDINBURGH | SCOTLAND

The Forth Bridge, spanning the Firth of Forth estuary, is an iron marvel of civil engineering, renowned for its distinctive red color. Held together by eight million rivets, the bridge requires regular repainting to protect against rust caused by sea salt carried on strong winds.

BEAUTIFUL

LENGTH 2,224 ft HEIGHT 492 ft YEAR OPENED 1980

Ganter Bridge

VALAIS | SWITZERLAND

Designed by civil engineer Christian Menn, the Ganter Bridge is a striking reinforced concrete structure set in a picturesque landscape. Its unique geometric shape is defined by cable stays embedded in concrete 'sails,' which support its exceptionally thin deck.

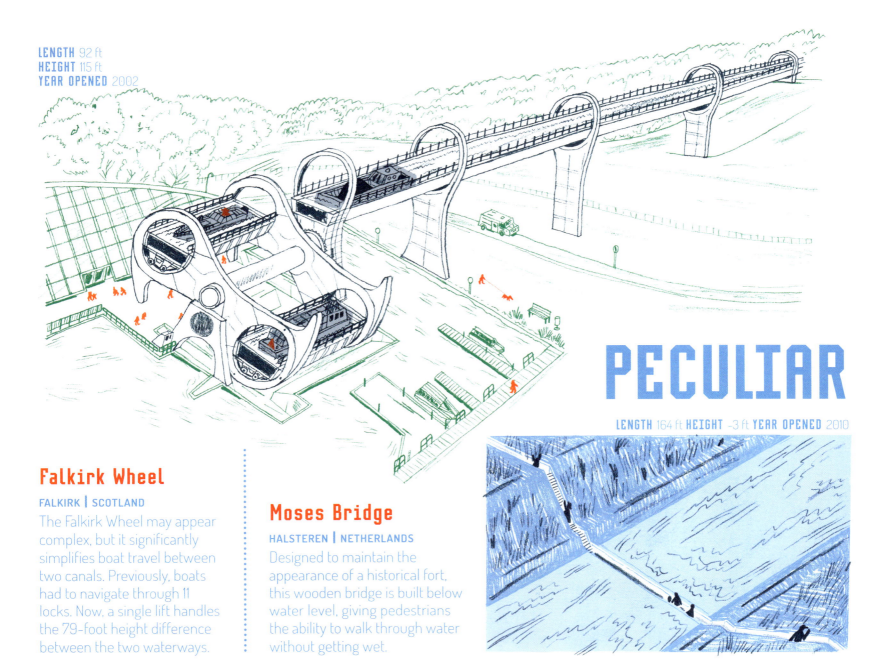

LENGTH 92 ft
HEIGHT 115 ft
YEAR OPENED 2002

PECULIAR

LENGTH 164 ft HEIGHT -3 ft YEAR OPENED 2010

Falkirk Wheel

FALKIRK | SCOTLAND

The Falkirk Wheel may appear complex, but it significantly simplifies boat travel between two canals. Previously, boats had to navigate through 11 locks. Now, a single lift handles the 79-foot height difference between the two waterways.

Moses Bridge

HALSTEREN | NETHERLANDS

Designed to maintain the appearance of a historical fort, this wooden bridge is built below water level, giving pedestrians the ability to walk through water without getting wet.

DANGEROUS

Hussaini Hanging Bridge

GILGIT-BALTISTAN | PAKISTAN

Many bridges are dangerous and poorly maintained, but the Hussaini Bridge attracts tourists seeking a thrill. Spanning the raging River Hunza, the bridge is made of 472 wooden slats, though many are now missing. Due to its precarious sway, it is recommended that no more than seven people cross at a time.

LENGTH 660 ft HEIGHT 50-100 ft
YEAR OPENED 1977

GREAT BRIDGES WE HAVEN'T MENTIONED YET

Laguna Garzón Bridge

MALDONADO–ROCHA DEPARTMENT | URUGUAY

This unusual circular-shaped bridge was designed to force drivers to slow down as they go over it.

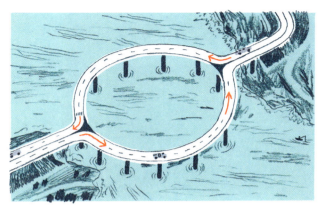

LENGTH 1,060 ft **YEAR OPENED** 2015

Øresund Bridge

COPENHAGEN, DENMARK | MALMÖ, SWEDEN

The longest and boldest of several bridges that cross the Denmark–Sweden border, the Øresund Bridge connects the two countries by motorway and – below this – by rail. It is under constant surveillance by 256 cameras, and marine plants and crustaceans thrive on its 51 piers that go deep underwater.

border

LENGTH 4.9 miles **HEIGHT** 187 ft **YEAR OPENED** 2000

Eshima Ohashi Bridge

MATSUE | JAPAN

Eshima Ohashi Bridge, often called the world's steepest bridge, is not for the faint-hearted. Its dramatic incline appears more daunting from a distance than up close.

LENGTH 5,577 ft **HEIGHT** 144 ft **YEAR OPENED** 2004

Chengyang Wind and Rain Bridge

CHENGYANG | CHINA

This covered wooden bridge, built without a single nail, combines elements of a bridge, Chinese pavilion, and veranda. It serves as an important connection between two villages and is a dreamy recreational spot set in a captivating, misty forest landscape.

Kapellbrücke

LUCERNE | SWITZERLAND

Kapellbrücke, the oldest bridge in Europe, is renowned for its unique triangular paintings. In 1993, a fire almost entirely destroyed the bridge. Fortunately, it was quickly restored to preserve its historical significance.

LENGTH 673 ft **HEIGHT** 113 ft **YEAR OPENED** 1333

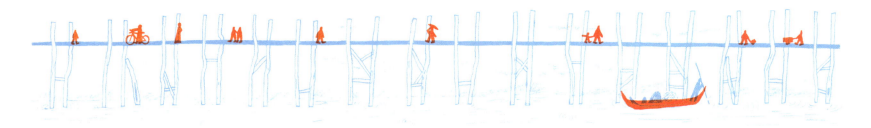

U Bein Bridge

LENGTH 3,937 ft **HEIGHT** various
YEAR OPENED 1850

AMARAPURA | MYANMAR

Standing since 1850, U Bein Bridge is the oldest and longest teak bridge in the world. Teak is highly resistant to changing weather, mould, and termites. The bridge can become crowded, and since it has no railings, users must navigate carefully around cyclists, children, vendors, and Buddhist monks.

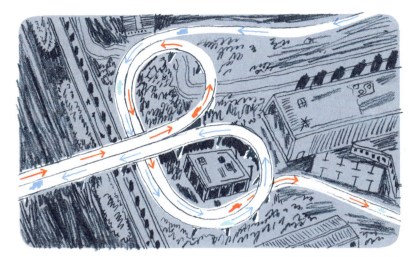

LENGTH 5,761 ft **YEAR OPENED** 2000

Si-o-Se-Pol Bridge

LENGTH 978 ft
YEAR OPENED 1602

ISFAHAN | IRAN

With 33 arches, Si-o-Se-Pol Bridge is the longest and most beautiful bridge on the River Zayanderud. The arches regulate the river's flow and serve as a dam. It is especially enchanting at night when illuminated, resembling a scene from a fairy tale.

Lótus Bridge

MACAU | CHINA

The Lótus Bridge ingeniously manages the transition between left-sided driving in Macau and right-sided driving in China, ensuring a smooth switch for drivers as they cross the border. Ingenious!

LENGTH 211 ft **HEIGHT** 33 ft **YEAR OPENED** 1916

Place your favourite **BRIDGE** here!

Q'eswachaka Rope Bridge

LENGTH 98 ft **HEIGHT** 92 ft
YEAR OPENED Unknown (renewed annually)

HUINCHIRI | PERU

This hand-woven grass rope bridge, originally built in Inca times, is renewed annually by locals. Women harvest and braid the grass into sturdy ropes, which are then handed to the men who dismantle the old bridge and construct a new one in just three days. Despite a modern footbridge nearby, this traditional ritual continues every year.

How did we get all these **BRIDGES?**
FIND YOUR WAY to discover the answer.

Start here

START

End here

END

Next up:
HISTORY

BRIDGES ACROSS THE AGES

It's hard to imagine a world without bridges, but for many centuries, people had to live without them. Change came slowly at first as people learned and made new discoveries. Even though they faced failures, builders kept trying to find better ways to construct bridges. Bridges helped civilizations explore new territories and allowed towns and cities to grow. With technological progress and new materials, bridges became taller and longer. Many bridges have stood strong through the ages and have even been part of important historical events.

But let's start at the

BEGINNING...

The opening of a new bridge has always been an important event.

CITY + BRIDGE = BIGGER CITY

TIMES change, BRIDGES remain.

At first, the only bridges were made by nature.

I SEE!

Nature taught humans **HOW TO DO IT.**

HUMANS BUILT BRIDGES
with the materials closest to hand.

PILE BRIDGES made of wood.

ROPE BRIDGES
woven from grasses and plants.

VAULT!

VAULTS were an invention that enabled bridges to become stronger and bigger structures.

STONE BRIDGES made of strong, resilient, readily available material, which remained popular until the 19th century.

1300–1190 BCE

1000 BCE

ARKADIKO BRIDGE, Greece
WORLD'S OLDEST SURVIVING BRIDGE

TARR STEPS, England

THE HELLESPONT WILL BE HUMBLED...

Xerxes I

482 BCE

The PONTOON BRIDGES of Persian kings Darius and Xerxes made history with their length and boldness.

The historian Herodotus described the city of Babylon.

Antiquity

PONTIFEX MAXIMUS

The Romans considered a bridge to be sacred. A group of **PONTIFFS** (priests) directed its building.

Roman buildings were durable thanks to ROMAN CONCRETE, which was made of quicklime, volcanic ash, and seawater.

The ARCHES were built on wooden formwork and solid STONE PIERS set in sumps.

WE CAN BUILD STONE COLUMNS.

WE CAN EVEN BUILD ARCHES.

THEY'RE WELL DRESSED *AND* THEY CAN BUILD!

WE CAN WORK IRON.

Etruscan

??? Roman

Having learned from the Greeks and Etruscans, the Romans build one of the world's greatest empires.

De Architectura × 10

30 BCE

VITRUVIUS writes a book on architecture.

The Romans are all about

INNOVATION.

105

TRAJAN'S BRIDGE over the Danube at 3,724 feet is **THE LARGEST BRIDGE** of its time.

YOU'VE GOT TEN DAYS TO DO IT, LADS!

Julius Caesar

55 BCE

CAESAR'S BRIDGE OVER THE RHINE
The 1,411-foot bridge was built in only 10 days!

Rome's emperors built bridges all over the *EMPIRE.*

117

Roman water mains

aqueduct

AQUEDUCTS carried water to cities from distant places. Set at a slight slope, they were several stories high and made of huge arches of stone or brick.

476

The **EASTERN ROMAN (BYZANTINE) EMPIRE** develops undisturbed. And they build great bridges!

605

ANJI BRIDGE IN CHINA is the world's oldest surviving arch bridge.

The **WESTERN ROMAN EMPIRE** falls. Now in decline, Europe is slow to make progress.

Roman bridges go to ruin and are dismantled for material. Few new bridges are built.

I'VE HAD ENOUGH OF THIS!

LET'S START BUILDING PROPER BRIDGES AGAIN!

800

The great monarch Charlemagne restores the importance of bridges.

A BRIDGE MUST BE:
- of hard-wearing material
- wide enough
- made with solid foundations
- well maintained
- fitted with railings and towers

818

The **BRIDGE CODE** of Louis the Pious and his principles for bridge construction states:

Stones are fitted together with MORTAR, QUICKLIME, and METAL FASTENERS.

The **BRIDGE-BUILDING BROTHERHOOD** of Avignon expands construction of bridges throughout Europe.

1209

For centuries, the Old London Bridge is the only stone bridge over the Thames.

1298

Marco Polo travels the world and is the first European to describe life in Asia.

As it is gradually built on, it becomes overloaded, damaged and dangerous.

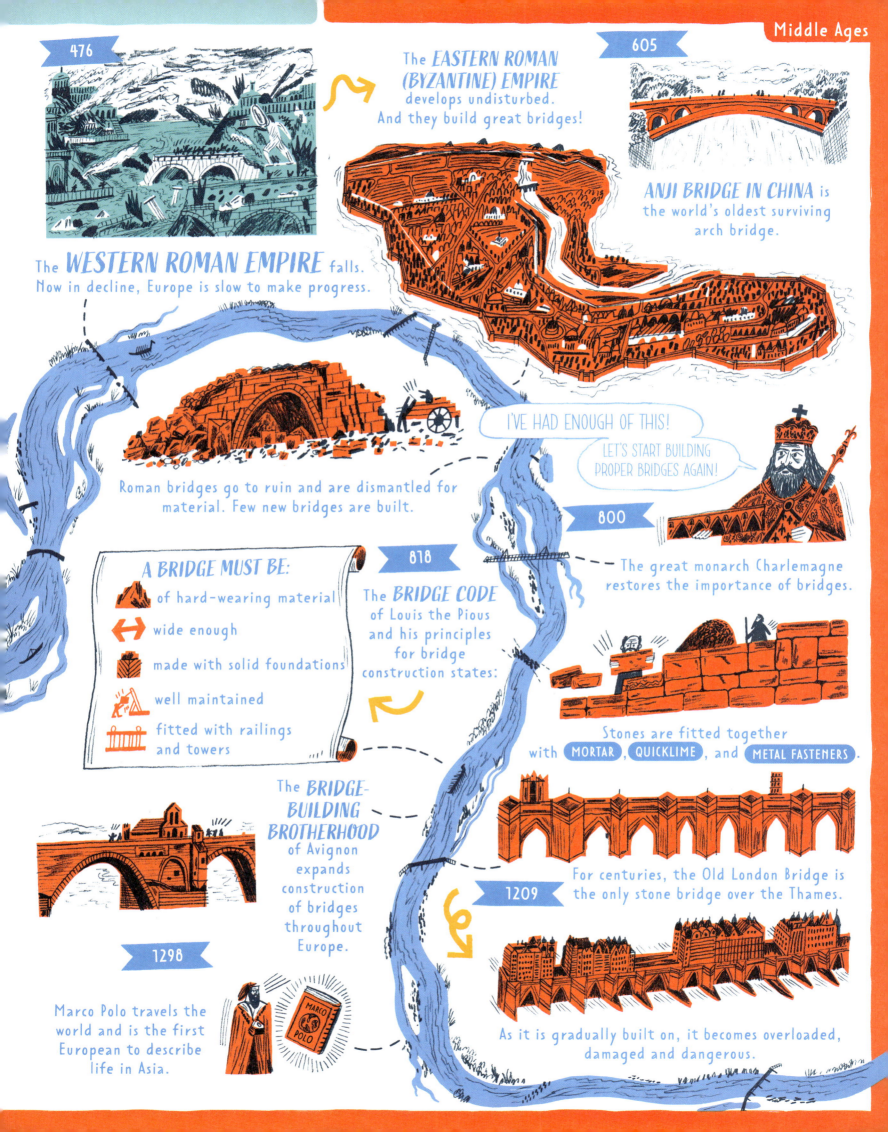

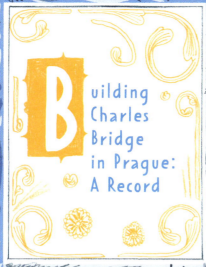

Building Charles Bridge in Prague: A Record

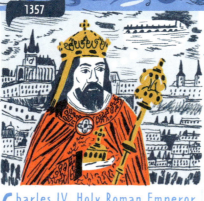

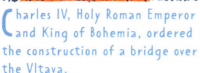

Charles IV, Holy Roman Emperor and King of Bohemia, ordered the construction of a bridge over the Vltava.

The bridge was built near the site of the old Judith Bridge, which was badly damaged in a flood. Construction followed 15 years of preparation, involving breaking stones, binding materials, and planning.

The work began with the most complex parts: the supporting pillars. Each was built in a separate pit formed by several rows of stakes and filled with clay. Water was drained from the finished sump by a pump driven by a water wheel. The foundation for the bridge tower was then laid in the space this created.

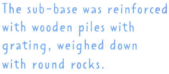

The sub-base was reinforced with wooden piles with grating, weighed down with round rocks.

Each pillar was set in place, totalling 15 pillars (to create 16 arches).

After construction of two or more pillars, bays for the vaults were built between them. For work on the vaults, wooden scaffolding was made and blocks of sandstone laid on it to create an arch.

The pillars and vault bays were walled in at the level of the bridge deck, after which the cobbles were laid.

Work on the bridge took many years. It became a new city center and Prague's pride and joy. Crowds passed from one bank to the other, and business was brisk. Charles Bridge, as it came to be known, helped Prague to grow. Still standing today, it has become an emblem of the city.

For a more detailed look at Charles Bridge, see page:

23

Pont Neuf in Paris is the **FIRST BRIDGE WITH PAVEMENTS** for pedestrians.

1609

ISAAC NEWTON explains gravity, by which we know that everything is pulled towards the Earth – an important discovery for bridge-builders.

1747

1687

A NATIONAL SCHOOL FOR BRIDGES AND ROADS is established in Paris, a big step for bridge engineering.

1574

Bridges are built in **LUXURY MATERIALS**, such as the marble Bridge of Sighs in Venice.

1615

Fausto Veranzio makes the first design for a SUSPENSION BRIDGE in his work **MACHINAE NOVAE**.

The human world is in tumult. Natural sciences, physics, and mathematics develop. Printing is invented. Copernicus declares the Sun to be the center of the Universe. *IT IS A TIME OF GREAT CHANGE.*

Beginning of the

MODERN ERA

Christopher Columbus reaches the Americas...

LEONARDO DA VINCI designs a self-supporting bridge that can be quickly built and dismantled without nails or cords.

The Inca build extra-strong SUSPENSION BRIDGES from grasses.

1492

...and the world known to Europeans becomes bigger.

1521

TENOCHTITLAN, center of the Aztec Empire that is built on islands, is destroyed by Spanish conquistadors.

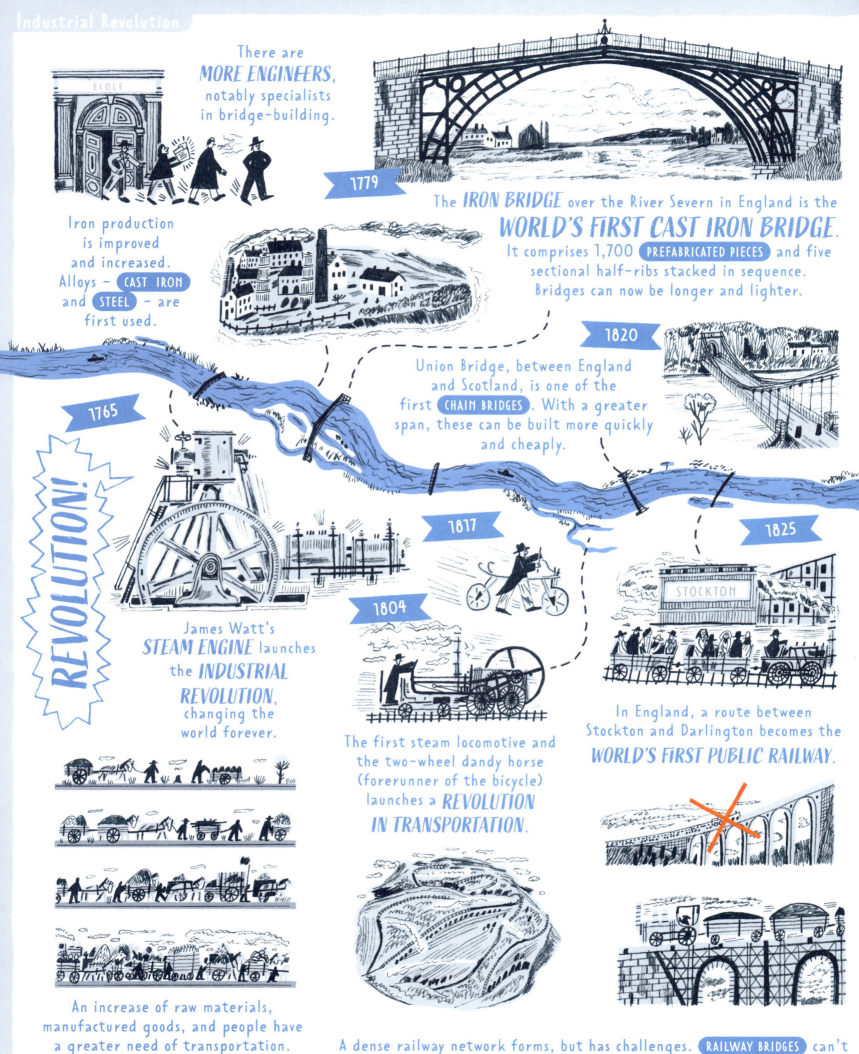

There are **MORE ENGINEERS**, notably specialists in bridge-building.

Iron production is improved and increased. Alloys – CAST IRON and STEEL – are first used.

1779

The **IRON BRIDGE** over the River Severn in England is the **WORLD'S FIRST CAST IRON BRIDGE**. It comprises 1,700 PREFABRICATED PIECES and five sectional half-ribs stacked in sequence. Bridges can now be longer and lighter.

1820

Union Bridge, between England and Scotland, is one of the first CHAIN BRIDGES. With a greater span, these can be built more quickly and cheaply.

1765

REVOLUTION!

James Watt's **STEAM ENGINE** launches the **INDUSTRIAL REVOLUTION**, changing the world forever.

1817

1804

The first steam locomotive and the two-wheel dandy horse (forerunner of the bicycle) launches a **REVOLUTION IN TRANSPORTATION**.

1825

STOCKTON

In England, a route between Stockton and Darlington becomes the **WORLD'S FIRST PUBLIC RAILWAY**.

An increase of raw materials, manufactured goods, and people have a greater need of transportation. More roads and bridges are required.

A dense railway network forms, but has challenges. RAILWAY BRIDGES can't handle steep inclines and must be robust enough to carry heavy trains.

Joseph Aspdin patents **PORTLAND CEMENT.** It hardens well and fixes materials together.

1824

Thomas Telford

MY BRIDGE OVER THE NIAGARA IS PHENOMENAL...

...BUT I'M PLANNING SOMETHING BIGGER.

MY BRIDGE OVER THE MENAI STRAIT SHOWED THE WAY.

MY FATHER AND I BUILD LOCOMOTIVES... AND BRIDGES, OF COURSE.

WE'RE ALL INNOVATORS, THAT'S FOR SURE.

THE FUTURE IS IN LIGHTWEIGHT, WELDED STRUCTURES.

Robert Stephenson

John Augustus Roebling

Isambard Kingdom Brunel

Gustave Eiffel

The world is teeming with **OUTSTANDING ENGINEERS**, many of whom advance bridge-building in new ways.

CONCRETE IS HERE

1826

Menai Suspension Bridge, Wales

DISCOVERIES AND NEW DEVELOPMENTS work wonders. Bridge production is now faster and easier, while bridges are longer, safer, and more stable.

rivets

1867

Joseph Monier patents **CONCRETE REINFORCED WITH STEEL.** Now it is resistant to tension as well as pressure.

TRUSSES become popular. Made of metal, they are composed of different shapes fixed together by recurring elements.

Warren truss

Pratt truss

Petit truss

1830

America builds a railway. Multi-story `'MATCHSTICK' BRIDGES` are quick and cheap to build.

1855

Henry Bessemer **IMPROVES STEEL PRODUCTION.** Steel now melts faster and is of higher quality for use in larger, more complex structures.

STATICS, concerned with the action of force and maintenance of balance in built structures, becomes a separate branch of engineering.

THE STORY OF THE BROOKLYN BRIDGE

In the 1850s...

New York

Brooklyn

When the river freezes in winter, ships full of passengers can get stuck in the ice for hours. This situation is not sustainable.

ENOUGH! I'LL BUILD A BRIDGE.

Hundreds of boats and ships criss-cross the East River daily. There is no other way to travel between New York (Manhattan) and Brooklyn.

John A. Roebling, an innovative engineer and suspension bridge expert, believes he has the perfect solution. But the East River is a tough nut to crack – no one has ever attempted to build such a long bridge before!

FRIENDS, YOU SEE BEFORE YOU THE WORLD'S LONGEST BRIDGE AND THE FIRST MADE WITH STEEL ROPES.

IT'S UP TO YOU NOW, SON!

Preparations are lengthy and drawn-out: it takes over ten years to get the green light for Roebling's bridge. Finally, in June 1869, approval is granted.

John Roebling never gets to see his greatest work: less than a month later, he dies. Construction of the bridge passes to his son Washington, also an experienced engineer.

The biggest problem is the pillars, which must be very robust for such a great span, but also have to be built on the bed of a deep, fast-flowing river.

HOW DO WE BUILD THE PILLARS?

WE'LL USE CAISSONS. COMPRESSED AIR WILL STOP THEM FROM BEING FLOODED, SO WE CAN LAY THE FOUNDATIONS.

THEY'LL BE HUGE. 167 BY 105 FEET.

A CAISSON WORKS LIKE THIS:

1 First built on the bank, a wooden caisson is tugged to the bridge site and sunk to the bottom.

2 Inside the caisson, workers dig out the subsurface layers of soil and rock, while others build a stone pier on top. As they work, the caisson sinks deeper into the riverbed.

3 When it hits the bedrock below, the caisson is filled with concrete and becomes the foundation of the pier.

THIS IS A REAL DRAG.

IT'S TOO MUCH PRESSURE.

Those working in the caissons soon have health problems, including joint pain, muscle spasms, and loss of consciousness. Washington Roebling, too, falls seriously ill.

CAISSON DISEASE IS CAUSED BY EFFECTS OF DECOMPRESSION ON THE BODY.

WHAT ARE WE GOING TO DO, EMILY?

DON'T WORRY. I'LL FINISH THE BRIDGE.

Work in the caissons is terrible. Workers enter on a ladder through a closed chamber. Excavated material is conveyed upward in a shaft with the aid of a scoop.

Intrepid Emily Roebling assumes the duties of chief engineer, dealing with city hall, managing the workers, and supervising construction.

The tower on the Brooklyn side was finished in 1875, and the Manhattan side a year later. Now, they could set up the four main cables. Each cable is 16 inches wide and made of 5,282 wires in 19 strands. These main cables stretch between the towers, supporting the bridge and holding it up.

NOW WE'LL TIGHTEN THE MAIN CABLES...

AREN'T YOU AFRAID?

WE SAILORS HAVE NO FEAR OF HEIGHTS.

The cables were assembled at the site, stretched back and forth between the banks over the towers, and then bundled into the main cables.

...AND HANG THE BRIDGE.

The deck is held by 1,520 steel suspender cables.

Diagonal suspender cables are added from the towers to increase stability.

WE DID IT!

HURRAH!

HURRAH!

After 14 arduous years, the bridge has its grand opening on May 24, 1883. Thousands of people attend, including US President Chester A. Arthur and the Mayor of New York. Emily Roebling is the first to cross the bridge. From that day on, the flow of traffic between Brooklyn and Manhattan has never stopped.

THE FIRST
GIANT

The Brooklyn Bridge changed the idea of what a bridge could be. It remained the world's largest for many years.

Madison Street Bridge, Chicago, USA

1922

1919

Quebec Bridge, Canada

Howrah Bridge, Kolkata, India

1943

BRIDGE BOOM

Now bridge-building is even more complex!

Many bridge types are built, including suspension, cantilever, and bascule. **BRIDGES GET LONGER AND BOLDER.**

1909

Manhattan Bridge, New York, USA

1937

Each main cable of the Golden Gate Bridge is 36 inches thick and has 27,572 strands of wire.

INTERNATIONAL ORANGE – a special, iconic color that makes a bridge easier to see in fog.

1886

Carl Benz presents the **FIRST MOTOR CAR**...

1945

Throughout two world wars, bridges become **STRATEGIC POINTS**. One of the most famous battles over a bridge is fought at Remagen in March 1945.

... which **CHANGES THE WORLD.** Bridges must now bear greater loads and be even safer.

1926

1900

The decorative style of the turn of the century is reflected in its bridges, such as Pont Alexander III in Paris.

Eugène Freyssinet builds the Plougastel concrete arch bridge. He devises a way of improving concrete by prestress and his method is patented.

CONCRETE CAN BE SHAPED
by pouring it into a mold.
Wonders of construction follow!

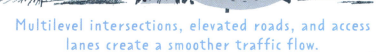

Multilevel intersections, elevated roads, and access lanes create a smoother traffic flow.

× 150 = BRIDGE

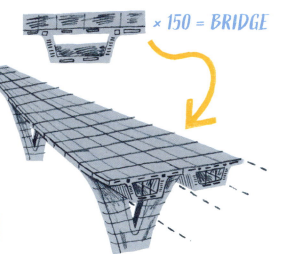

Clever computer programs, the work of many specialist professionals, help with bridge design.

SEGMENTAL BRIDGES
allow factory-made pieces to be taken to a site and fitted there.

2001

In the 2000s, pedestrian bridges became more important. **FOOTBRIDGES** like Santiago Calatrava's El Puente de la Mujer in Buenos Aires are very popular.

Many bridges are damaged or destroyed during the Second World War. All must be repaired or rebuilt.

Construction is made easier with **MODERN MACHINES.**

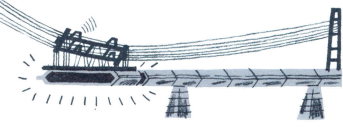

REINFORCED CONCRETE and PRESTRESSED CONCRETE look similar because both use steel bars for reinforcement. However, prestressed concrete is stronger because the steel bars are tensioned before the concrete is poured, providing extra strength.

Riccardo Morandi's bridge over Lake Maracaibo in Venezuela is around 5.4 miles long. The structure is made of prestressed concrete.

1962

41

1998

AKASHI KAIKYO BRIDGE
During its construction, the Akashi Kaikyo Bridge in Japan faced an earthquake, causing the two main towers to move apart by about 3 feet.

BRIDGES AS A DESTINATION
Bridges aren't just about crossing from one place to another; they have become destinations themselves. Modern bridges are often designed to attract visitors.

Modern bridges are more than just paths for crossing – they offer great views and showcase new designs and technologies.

2010

2020

2023

TEXTILE CONCRETE
– a new, lighter, thinner, eco-friendly reinforced concrete. A bridge using this material was built in Albstadt, Germany.

Twist Bridge, Norway, is a bridge, museum, and sculpture in one.

Bridges are now for stopping on as well as crossing, and can have a park or recreation area.

Future challenges for designing bridges involve supporting high-speed maglev train travel while being resistant to seismic activities and harsh weather conditions...

... as well as considering how bridges can be used to make energy.

2021

3D PRINTED BRIDGE
Queen Maxima Bridge, Amsterdam

RAPID ADVANCES IN BRIDGE-BUILDING
Highest, longest... No bridge stays at the top of the list for long!

WHAT DOES THE FUTURE HOLD FOR BRIDGES?

HOW TO BUILD A BRIDGE

Unless you're building a plank bridge across a stream with a few wooden boards, a hammer and some nails, bridge-building is hard work. With a big bridge, every last detail is important: the design and construction must be well plotted and planned, with every part properly counted and measured. A bridge must stand firm to be safe, yet still allow for movement due to various forces, so there are many important steps before, during, and after its construction.

1. PREPARATION

This is done at a desk as well as on site. Many specialists are involved, notably engineers, stress-strain analysts, architects, water resource managers, and geologists. All make plans and give advice. The chief designer incorporates the best ideas into drawings and the architectural plans are born! Now we know the dimensions of each part of the bridge, the load it must bear, what material will be used where, the length of railings and where they will be attached to the structure, and more.

2. CONSTRUCTION

It's time to leave the office and head to the building site. Excavators, concrete mixers, and other special machines arrive. After years of preparation, the ground is broken. How a bridge is built depends on its design, demands of the terrain, and choice of materials. Bridge construction is technically demanding, must meet strict requirements of safety and functionality, and may take several years. The bridge grows gradually through the hard work of many people.

3. INSPECTION

The bridge is up, but the work continues. Before it can be opened, it must undergo a thorough inspection. Everything is checked. Can it bear the necessary load? Can it withstand vibrations from crossing vehicles? Do the lighting and drainage systems function properly? Are all the traffic signs in the right place? These final checks ensure the bridge is safe and ready for use. Bridges continue to be inspected even after they are opened to make sure there is no damage and they remain safe.

WHY DOESN'T HE SWIM ACROSS?

HE'S ALWAYS HAD HIS OWN STYLE!

FOLLOW THESE RULES:

→ Plan well

→ Find the right people
CROSS & BOND Ltd.

→ Respect lessons from history

→ Be brave and have a vision

LEARNING FROM MISTAKES

Over the years, many bridges have sadly collapsed. This can happen because of design mistakes, human error, or natural disasters. Bridges falling down or being destroyed is something that has happened in the past and still happens today. Even though it is unfortuante when a bridge falls, engineers learn important lessons from it and improve their designs over time.

UNDERESTIMATING THE WIND

> COMPUTER SIMULATION CAN CHECK HOW EXTERNAL FORCES ACT ON A STRUCTURE.

1940

Tacoma Narrows Bridge

TACOMA | USA

This bridge collapsed four months after it was opened due to flaws in its aerodynamic design. The bridge's solid sides didn't allow the wind to pass over the deck, causing it to catch the wind and sway until it collapsed. Miraculously, no one was killed in the incident.

> EXPECT THE UNEXPECTED AND MINIMIZE THE VULNERABILITY OF THE STRUCTURE.

NEGLECTED MAINTENANCE

1807

> BRIDGES MUST UNDERGO REGULAR INSPECTION AND REPAIR.

Eitai-bashi Bridge

TOKYO | JAPAN

This old bridge between two villages was in bad shape for a long time, but nobody fixed it. During a festival, it collapsed, and 1,400 people sadly drowned in the water below.

OVERLOAD

1297

Stirling Bridge

STIRLING | SCOTLAND

English and Scottish armies clashed on this bridge during the First War of Scottish Independence. The bridge collapsed under their collective weight, resulting in many deaths.

> PERFORM REGULAR LOAD TESTS AND DO NOT OVERLOAD THE BRIDGE.

BAD WEATHER

1980

Sunshine Skyway Bridge

ST. PETERSBURG | USA

During a storm, a large freighter hit a support pier of the bridge, causing cars to fall from the damaged structure and killing 35 people. The piers were not well-protected against such impacts. Today, a modern bridge stands in place of the original.

POOR CONSTRUCTION

1907 and 1916

> THOROUGH PLANS, CALCULATIONS AND CHECKING OF MATERIALS ARE KEY.

Quebec Bridge

LÉVIS | CANADA

This bridge collapsed twice while under construction. The first collapse – in which 76 workers died – was due to a major flaw in the design. The second occurred when the central section of the bridge disintegrated due to faulty material.

WHAT EVERY BRIDGE MUST WITHSTAND

A bridge might stand on rough terrain, straddle a vast abyss, or be battered by wild winds or mighty waves. Yet stand it must. A bridge is a security, a servant and, of course, a hero. A good bridge-builder has to consider many forces and eventualities to ensure a bridge remains steady, reliable, and safe.

ITS OWN WEIGHT

First and foremost, a bridge must carry its own weight, i.e. that of its structure and materials.

LOAD

It must take the weight of all vehicles, pedestrians and/or trains crossing at any one time. For safety's sake, it should be able to withstand more than it needs to.

NATURAL ELEMENTS

It must be resistant to gales, flooding, and torrential rain. Natural elements are highly diverse and geographically distinct. In some parts of the world, bridges must survive earthquakes; in others, extreme fluctuations in temperature.

PREPARE FOR THE UNEXPECTED...

There's no predicting what might happen in the future, so a good bridge-builder should prepare for everything, including:

- fire
- people crowding on one side of the bridge
- being struck by a vehicle
- a group of overexcited children
- a vehicle pile-up
- a demonstration or marathon with many participants
- any other unusual situations

PREVENTING A COLLAPSE

First and foremost, a builder must know about the many forces that act upon all structures – including bridges – because these forces can affect their stability and strength. To prevent a building or bridge from collapsing, it must be designed so that its individual parts carry and absorb these various forces correctly.

COUNT WITH GRAVITY

Gravity pulls everyone and everything groundward, thus creating weight. The heavier the bridge, the greater the gravitational force acting upon it.

KNOW ABOUT THE SUBSURFACE

What goes on underground – where the bridge's foundations will be – is crucial for stability and functionality. Does the subsurface contain solid rock or clay? Does groundwater flow through it? These questions, and many more, must be answered and addressed in the design.

RESPECT THE MATERIAL

Materials behave in different ways. Metal and concrete (the most common materials in bridge-building) are affected by temperature, so can shrink in winter and expand in summer. This must be appreciated and prepared for.

MASTER TENSION AND COMPRESSION

These basic forces will act on the structure, so the chief engineer must check that they are transferred or spread across the bridge so that no part is overloaded. Each bridge carries these forces differently and the chief engineer must know how to manage them.

COMPRESSION

TENSION

beam bridge

arch bridge

suspension bridge

cable-stayed bridge

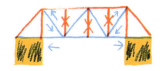
truss bridge

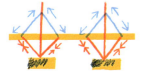
cantilever bridge

HOW IS IT DONE?

Bridge engineers study at specialized schools. There is a lot to learn, so they study for a long time. Then they know what to watch out for and how to deal with different situations – but they have some help to do this.

SOFTWARE AND PROGRAMMERS

These are crucial for good bridge design. Computer software creates detailed 3D models and technical drawings; it calculates load, analyzes structure, and simulates different conditions, such as extreme high winds or earth tremors. Such helpers are invaluable.

WIND TUNNEL

This apparatus tests and examines the aerodynamic properties of structures, including bridges. Fans create air flow so that its effect on a model can be monitored. This removes the need to conduct difficult experiments in real environments.

FINAL STRESS TEST

An essential step in the verification of a bridge's safety before it is put into service. During the final stress test, the bridge is slightly overloaded to confirm that it is as strong and stable as it should be.

SLIDING BRIDGE CLOSURES

Covering the expansion joints, closures allow for slight movement in the structure to counter temperature change. Most closures are scissor-shaped and open and close as required. As they must be water- and corrosion-proof, they are commonly made of steel. Without them, the bridge's roadway would crack, damaging the structure and affecting its stability.

BEARINGS, DAMPERS, AND PENDULUMS

Bearings help a load-bearing structure react to movement in its parts and transfer load. Dampers reduce vibration on the bridge caused by traffic. Pendulums balance the effects of high winds and earth tremors.

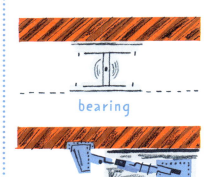

bearing

damper

pendulum

ROADWAY DRAINAGE

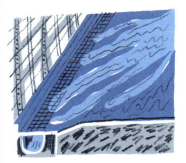

Without drainage, water would sit on the bridge, damaging its material and structure, making it dangerous for the user.

LET'S BUILD!

Now that we know how it's done, it's time to build! The construction site is a fascinating place filled with people, machines, and bridge parts, where the action never stops. Work is coordinated so that everything is connected logically, just like a well-functioning machine. Everyone has their role and knows how to perform it. Meanwhile, the bridge grows in height, width, length, and depth.

Diver

Helps with preparation and inspection of parts underwater.

Geologist

Examines the subsurface at the site and advises on how to make the foundations safe.

Architect

Plans the bridge's appearance, designs its structure, produces technical drawings of it, and supervises its construction.

Client
Commissions the building work and pays for it. With public construction work – as is commonly the case with bridges – the client is a city or regional authority.

Site manager
Manages the workers and ensures that work goes smoothly.

Workforce
The most numerous group at the site. Surveyors, diggers, carpenters, masons, drivers (of excavators, trucks, and cranes), machine operators, concrete finishers, strong workers with shovels, and snack providers make up a workforce that gets rapid results.

Chief engineer
Can be a team rather than one person. The role of chief engineer is key. They must ensure that the entire bridge is functional and safe.

CROSS & BOND Ltd.

FAMOUS BRIDGE-BUILDERS

EUGÈNE FREYSSINET
1879–1962
A French engineer who built ships, airship hangars, and bridges, he was a pioneer of prestressed concrete.

Thomas Telford
1757–1834

This Scottish architect, stonemason, and engineer of road and canal projects designed the world's first cast iron bridge (over the River Severn) and the ground-breaking Menai suspension bridge. Rather than relying on established methods, he tested properties of building materials, resulting in significant advances in engineering.

Apollodorus of Damascus
65 –130 CE

This Greek architect built the Pantheon in Rome and was a favorite of emperor Trajan. He built a bridge across the River Danube made of wood with stone pillars in 105 CE. This bridge supplied Roman legions fighting in Dacia, helping Trajan to a famous victory, which is depicted on Trajan's Column in Rome.

CHRISTIAN MENN
1927–2018

A Swiss engineer specialized in bridge-building who realized the potential of prestressed concrete and made significant innovations in bridge design.

Isambard Kingdom Brunel
1806–1859

A British engineer whose tunnels, ships, and bridges found solutions for many architectural and design challenges. While his Great Western Railway was under construction, he measured the line from London to Bristol himself. He designed the first propeller-driven, iron-hulled ship, the Royal Albert Bridge near Plymouth, and the Clifton Suspension Bridge in Bristol.

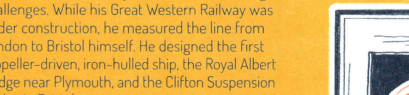

Santiago Calatrava
B. 1951

This Spanish architect has built bridges all over the world. He also designs railway stations, museums, and concert halls. His work is very distinctive in its asymmetrical designs made of white concrete and steel. Unusually elegant and airy, some of his buildings look as though they are about to take flight!

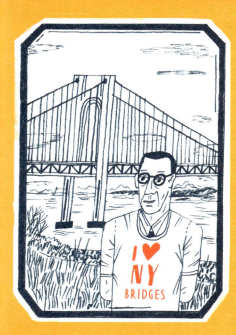

Othmar Ammann

1879–1965

This Swiss-American engineer spent most of his career in New York, where he designed six bridges. His George Washington Bridge was the first to cross the wild Hudson River. His masterpiece is the Verrazzano-Narrows Bridge, the traditional starting point of the New York City Marathon.

NORMAN FOSTER
B. 1935

This legendary British architect redesigned the Reichstag in Berlin, built a bridge to the Tate Modern gallery, and is the brains behind London's famous Gherkin building.

Gustave Eiffel

1832–1923

An icon of civil engineering whose name has been immortalized largely thanks to his 984-foot-high tower in Paris. But bridges were his masterpieces. He specialized in lattice girders, from which he built light, airy structures all over the world. A great example of his boldness and innovation is the Garabit viaduct in southern France.

ZAHA HADID
1950–2016

A fearless Iraqi-British architect who shunned right angles, her dynamic buildings are unmissable.

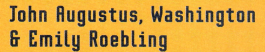

John Augustus, Washington & Emily Roebling

J.A. (1806–1869), W.R. (1837–1926), E.R. (1843–1903)

This father, son, and daughter-in-law trio built New York's iconic Brooklyn Bridge. John was a visionary engineer and immigrant from Germany who became a driving force of US construction. He made his name with a bold suspension over the raging Niagara River. Although he didn't live to see his greatest work, he was fortunate to have a talented son and daughter-in-law to complete it for him.

Ralph Modjeski

1861–1940

This Polish-American engineer studied in Europe before becoming America's greatest bridge-builder. In fixing the poorly designed Quebec Bridge, he created the longest truss span in the world. As well as building around 40 bridges over rivers in North America, he designed railroads and was a pioneer of the suspension bridge. His home was Chicago, where he was instrumental in teaching a new generation of bridge-builders.

JOSEPH STRAUSS
1870–1938

The American engineer who revolutionized the bascule bridge and designed the iconic Golden Gate Bridge in San Francisco.

EMBELLISHMENTS

Since a bridge is distinctive in and of itself, does it need anything else? Not always: often its shape, materials, remarkable design, or surroundings are enough. In the past, bridges were commonly adorned with statues and lavishly shaped railings in many colors. Although present-day bridge-building focuses on function and favors moderation and minimalism, architects and builders don't always shy away from unique design and embellishments.

STATUES can be both classical and modern.

MATERIALS give color and structure.

OTHER FEATURES include restaurants, towers, and even observation wheels.

ILLUMINATION

TEMPORARY DECORATION is practically anything, as it is removable.

RAILINGS can be minimalist, ornate, or something in between.

LOOKING AFTER A BRIDGE

The control center at the Øresund Bridge monitors the bridge 24 hours a day using 256 cameras and many staff.

Every bridge must be well cared for. If it isn't, it could get damaged or – at the very worst – collapse. For this reason, bridges are regularly inspected by specialists. How often these checks happen vary from bridge to bridge, as every bridge is different. Some must be under constant supervision.

What must be done:

- regular inspection of all parts of the bridge
- repair or replacement of damaged parts
- treatment of metal parts against corrosion
- inspection of structural stability and load bearing
- replacement of security lighting
- (in movable bridges) inspection and lubrication of systems

DAMAGE TO A BRIDGE must be reported.

BRIDGE LIFE

When we walk over a bridge, we often slow down or even stop without really thinking about it. We might look down at the water or the scenery around us. People stop to enjoy the view, tourists take photos, and runners catch their breath – all are connected by these special moments on the bridge.

PLAYING THE MAIN ROLE

A bridge isn't just a structure – it's an important and timeless theme filled with hidden meanings and symbolism. A bridge can fascinate and charm us with its beauty, drama, and photogenic qualities, whether at dawn or dusk. It is a place for a romantic encounter or a decisive battle. It's no wonder that it takes the lead role in so many works of art.

Bridges are adored by writers...

action

romance

drama

fairy tale

...and loved by filmmakers...

CINEMA

10:00	BRIDGE OF SPIES
13:00	THE BRIDGE AT REMAGEN
16:00	A BRIDGE TOO FAR
19:00	BRIDGE TO TERABITHIA
22:00	TROLL BRIDGE

Bridges play big roles in the movies! They are often used to symbolize key moments, like making tough decisions or facing challenges. In Steven Spielberg's film 'Bridge of Spies', a bridge is where spies from different countries are exchanged. In the fantasy film 'Troll Bridge', a bridge takes center stage as a brave character faces off against a troll.

...musicians...

SIMON & GARFUNKEL

...and visual artists.

Bridges also inspire many famous works of art! For example, the French artist, Claude Monet, painted a pretty bridge in his garden called '*The Japanese Bridge*' that makes you feel calm and peaceful when you look at it. Vincent van Gogh painted '*The Bridge at Arles*', showing what life was like in a small town. In art, bridges can mean starting something new or making connections, making them interesting to look at and think about.

POWERFUL SYMBOL

References to bridges can be found in everyday life, art, music, poetry, coats of arms, religion, and more. A bridge is a strong symbol because it is simple and easily understood by all. Its meaning may change a little from culture to culture, but for almost everyone, a bridge represents a connection, stability, and hope. This symbolism shows how important bridges are in linking people, places, and ideas.

Bridges appear as symbols of **unity** on Euro banknotes.

The bridge is a popular motif in company **logos**, especially for businesses involved in building bridges, food, and education.

A bridge appears in the **emblem** of many cities around the world.

Traditionally, enemies often make **peace** on bridges.

HOPE

A bridge can create feelings of excitement and fill us with good thoughts. It can represent positive change and a promise of something nice or interesting in the future.

STABILITY AND SECURITY

A bridge inspires confidence and a sense of security. It is solid, strong, and stays where it is, regardless of what is going on. Even when lashed by thunder and lightning, it will always be there to lead us to where we are going.

CONNECTION

A bridge connects, overcomes, and mediates. It joins everyone and everything. We often speak of a bridge between cultures, a bridge between generations, or a bridge between nations. It always brings us closer together and can overcome difference. As a mediator, it enables communication, helping people and groups understand each other.

RELATIONSHIPS

Metaphorically, we often talk of 'building bridges' (forming bonds) or 'burning our bridges' (breaking them and leaving everything behind), particularly within relationships and friendships, and between communities.

BUILDING

BURNING

PATH

As we go from one place to another, or travel toward a personal goal, a bridge helps us overcome obstacles with ease.

TRANSFORMATION

Crossing a bridge can represent the transformation of an individual, their mindset, or the achievement of a goal.

CROSSING

A bridge can also be a border or portal crossing over to the other world – for example from life to death.

FABLES & MYTHOLOGY

Bridges are important to many cultures and are commonly found in their stories. They may represent a turning point or, more commonly, a crossing to the afterlife.

Chinvat

In Zoroastrianism, an ancient religion from Persia, the Chinvat Bridge separates the world of the living from the world of the dead. Every soul must cross it after death; good people find it wide and easy to cross to a pleasant afterlife, while evil people face a narrow, difficult path and are pulled into the underworld.

Chinese mythology

I WONDER WHAT TO EXPECT.

Naihe

The Naihe Bridge, also known as the Bridge of Forgetfulness, leads to the underworld. Here, the goddess Meng Po serves a soup that erases a person's memory, allowing them to enter their new life without the burden of the past. However, evil souls are pushed into the river, preventing them from reincarnating.

As-Sirāt

Islam

As-Sirāt is a bridge from Islamic teachings that every soul must cross to enter paradise. Thinner than a hair and sharper than a sword, it spans the fires of Hell, where sinners are punished. Virtuous souls cross quickly and safely. This bridge is part of the final judgment.

Norse mythology

Gjallarbrú

In ancient Norse beliefs, to reach the afterlife known as Hel, one must cross Gjallarbrú, a bridge with a golden roof spanning the Gjöll river in the underworld.

Norse mythology

Bifrost

According to ancient Norse mythology, Bifrost is a burning rainbow bridge that connects Midgard (Earth) with Asgard (the realm of the gods).

MOVERS OF HISTORY

For much of human history, bridges have been places of crucial strategic significance that are fiercely protected but also intentionally destroyed. They have been the scene of countless great moments in history, including battles and meetings of leaders.

Battle of the Milvian Bridge

The night before the battle at the Milvian Bridge, Roman emperor Constantine I dreamed of a cross with the inscription: "In this sign, thou shalt conquer." Inspired, he had his army paint crosses on their shields. They won the battle at the bridge. Afterward, Constantine converted to Christianity and made it the Roman Empire's main religion.

312

Napoleon flees across the Berezina

In November 1812, Napoleon's army was retreating from Russia and needed to cross the Berezina River. They quickly built two secret bridges to escape, despite heavy attacks and many losses. This escape saved Napoleon's army, even though his failed Russian campaign marked his downfall.

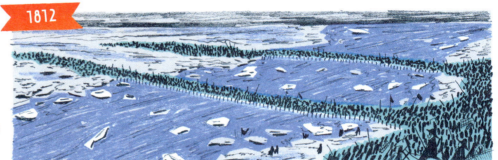

1812

Pegasus Bridge

Pegasus Bridge was an important part of World War II. On the night before the Normandy landings, British paratroopers captured the bridge from the Germans in just ten minutes. This allowed the Allies to move inland quickly and safely, helping them start their attack on German-occupied Europe.

1945

Three marches against racism

In March 1965, a peaceful march of 600 people, mostly Black Americans, was attacked by police on the Edmund Pettus Bridge in Selma, Alabama. This event, known as "Bloody Sunday," led to two more marches, attracting thousands of supporters led by Martin Luther King Jr. These efforts were crucial in the fight for civil rights, resulting in the Voting Rights Act which was passed in August 1965.

1965

MARTIN LUTHER KING JR.

Bridge between Europe and Asia

The first bridge between Europe and Asia was built by King Darius of Persia in 512 BCE, but it was temporary. It took nearly 2,000 years for a permanent bridge to be built. In 1973, the Bosphorus Bridge was opened, connecting the European and Asian parts of Istanbul. This bridge is not only useful but also a powerful symbol of unity. Today, there are three bridges over the Bosphorus river.

1973

Asia

Europe

A FEW MORE INTERESTING FACTS

MAINTAINING THE GOLDEN GATE BRIDGE

To keep it shiny for photos, but above all to ensure it is in perfect working order, the iconic Golden Gate Bridge is serviced every day by a maintenance team of around 50 workers. Metalworkers check the steel parts and make necessary repairs, while painters continually touch up the bridge's surfaces. This is work for an adventurer with a head for heights.

BRIDGEHEAD

A bridgehead is when an army secures a strong position inside enemy territory, creating a base for launching attacks and advancing further. A famous bridgehead was established by the Allies after the Normandy landings in World War II.

ANIMAL BRIDGES

Some animals are also masters of bridge-building. Take ants, which can build bridges with their bodies, covering great distances. Similarly, Darwin's bark spider, which lives in Madagascar, takes bridge-building to another level by weaving the strongest and largest known webs. With fibers up to 82 feet long, it can reach over a river or stream, making a perfect bridge to catch its prey.

BRIDGE PHOBIA

Not all people love bridges. Some are so afraid of them that rather than cross them, they take a more complicated route to go somewhere, avoiding them entirely. Fear of bridges, known as gephyrophobia, often affects people who have a fear of heights. It can come on suddenly, making it especially dangerous for drivers. Operators of some large bridges offer a service where a member of staff will drive you across the bridge in your own car.

BEWARE OF SOLDIERS

In 1850, a bridge collapsed while a group of French soldiers was marching across it. The regular rhythm of their footsteps caused the bridge to vibrate and collapse due to resonance. Today, when soldiers reach a bridge, their commander orders them to stop marching and walk across to prevent this from happening again.

BUILD LEONARDO'S BRIDGE

A self-supporting bridge can be really useful. Try building one at home with wooden skewers or ice pop sticks. You might find this skill helpful someday!

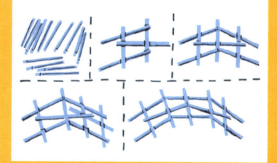

PONTIFEX MAXIMUS

In ancient Rome, pontiffs oversaw the construction of bridges. Today, the title Pontifex Maximus, which means 'builder of bridges,' refers to the highest representative of the Catholic Church. The Pope, as Pontifex Maximus, builds bridges between this world and the spiritual world through ideas and faith, rather than concrete.

SAINT JOHN OF NEPOMUK

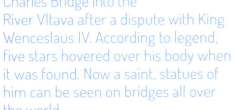

Saint John of Nepomuk is the patron saint of bridges. He is shown with five shining stars around his head, holding a cross and a palm branch. Once a church official, he was thrown from Prague's Charles Bridge into the River Vltava after a dispute with King Wenceslaus IV. According to legend, five stars hovered over his body when it was found. Now a saint, statues of him can be seen on bridges all over the world.

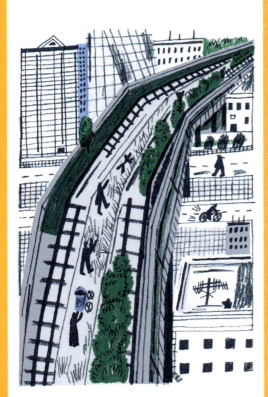

THE HIGH LINE, NEW YORK

Instead of demolishing a disused rail track in the heart of the city, New York transformed it into an elevated park known as the High Line. The park offers unique views of the city and features a diverse array of plants. Since its opening in 2009, the High Line has inspired cities around the world to rethink how they can repurpose neglected or abandoned spaces.

BRIDGES TO NOWHERE

Remnants of bridges can be found all over the world in fields, forests, or even ending in the middle of a lake. These bridges go from nowhere to nowhere. They may be relics of big plans that came to nothing. They may have ended their service but were never demolished. Or they may be leftovers from a construction where something went wrong. Dilapidated and surrounded by overgrown plants, they take on a charm of their own.

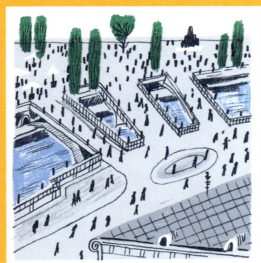

MULTIPLE BRIDGES NEXT TO EACH OTHER

In places with more than one bridge, each usually has a different purpose. For example, one might be for cars, another for trains, and another for walking. Sometimes, a new bridge is added because the first wasn't enough. Bridges can also be artistic. Jože Plečnik, a Slovenian architect, designed the famous Triple Bridge in Ljubljana, Slovenia, where pedestrians can take a different route every day!

BRIDGES FOR SPORTS

Bridges are great for sports. Marathons run over them, and their pillars can be used as climbing walls. Adrenaline lovers can even enjoy bungee jumping from bridges. In this sport, you jump off a bridge while attached to a safety cord, supervised by an instructor. Three, two, one, JUMP! The jumper flies off the edge and swings on the cord, feeling the thrill.

BRIDGES OF LAST RESORT

Every well-equipped medieval castle had a drawbridge – a sturdy, hinged structure that could be raised or lowered to protect against attackers. If a castle couldn't afford a drawbridge, it at least had a bridge that could be dismantled or easily destroyed. If an enemy made it in, defenders would head to an upper floor and cross this bridge to a defense tower, destroying the bridge behind them. We don't have reports on how long defenders stayed in the tower or what happened to them afterward.

NO TWO BRIDGES ARE THE SAME

We often only think of bridges as being something sturdy that we can walk across. But it would be boring if every bridge was a solid structure made of stone or steel. Other types of bridges appear in surprising places – such as at the dentist, a yoga class, or in concert halls!

AIRBRIDGE

This bridge is vitally important, yet invisible. An airbridge consists of airplanes flying to isolated places, delivering materials, food, or humanitarian aid to people who have no other way of getting them.

INSTRUMENT BRIDGES

Made of wood or metal, this crucial part of a stringed instrument holds the strings in the right position and at the right height so that their vibrations carry on the air to create sound – and music.

WE HAVE TO FIX IT WITH A DENTAL BRIDGE...

DENTAL BRIDGE

A dentist might put one of these in your mouth if you lose a tooth. The gap in the teeth is 'bridged' with an artificial tooth.

BRIDGE POSE IN YOGA

A yoga posture, known as an asana, is given a name based on what the pose looks like. The bridge pose, also known as a backbend, strengthens the arms and legs, exercises the lungs, stretches the abdomen, and is said to have a positive effect on mood.

BRIDGE PIERCING

A distinctive facial piercing where the skin on the bridge of the nose, between the eyes, has barbell or captive bead ring jewellery.

WHAT OTHER TYPES OF BRIDGES CAN YOU THINK OF?

ACKNOWLEDGEMENTS

For stimulating conversation, inspiration and helpful literature, I owe thanks to many people, especially: Osamu Okamura, Ivan Rous, Jakub Růžička, Martin Habina, Petr Štefek, Karel Filšák, Magdalena Deverová, Jakub Kynčl, Renata Ondráčková, Zdeněk Staszek, Štěpánka Sekaninová, Helena Haraštová, Radka Piro. MANY THANKS!

My special thanks go to Sir Norman Foster. The magnificent Millau Viaduct is pictured in the book with kind permission of Foster + Partners (fosterandpartners.com).

I thank my family and friends for their patience and support. Bridges have become an inseparable part of our lives.

Above all, I wish to thank my incredible colleagues, without whom this book would not look nearly as good. Jakub Bachorík and Roman Havlice are a dream team!

SOURCES AND FURTHER READING

Bridges are the subject of many books, articles, pictures and videos across all the world. We can talk about them with architects, engineers, parents, and friends about them. A bridge also makes a great destination for a day out. Scan the code to discover the resources used to write this book, and to learn even more about bridges.

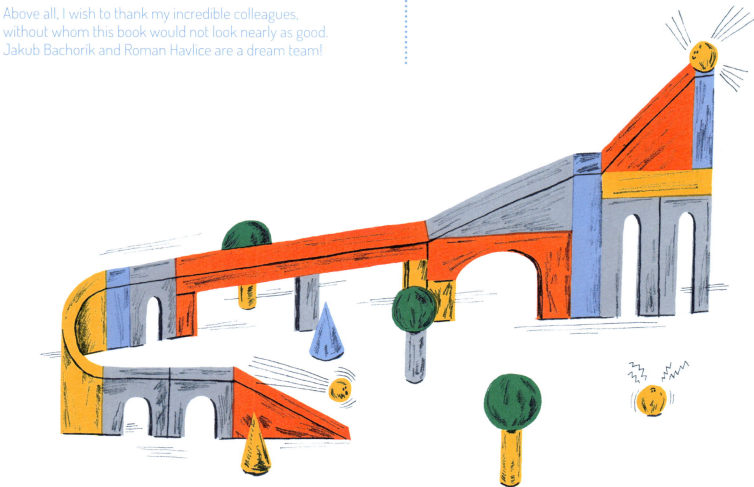

Published in the USA in 2025
by Post Wave Children's Books,
an imprint of Post Wave Publishing UK Ltd,
Runway East, 24–28 Bloomsbury Way, London, WC1A 2SN
www.postwavepublishing.com

First edition 2023
Published with permission of Albatros Media Group
Original title: *Bridges*
Written by Magda Gargulàková
Illustrated by Jakub Bachorik
Graphics by: Roman Havlice
Designed by: B4U Publishing, a member of Albatros Media Group

Printed and manufactured in China by Leo Paper Products,
Heshan, Guangdong, Oct 2024

Copyright © Albatros Media
Czech Republic, 2023
www.albatrosmedia.eu

10 9 8 7 6 5 4 3 2 1

ISBN: 979-8-89509-008-4

Printed in China

MIX
Paper | Supporting
responsible forestry
FSC® C020056

BRIDGES FROM THIS BOOK:

I'VE SEEN   I WANT TO SEE

A Akashi Kaikyo Bridge, Kobe, Japan

Alamillo Bridge, Seville, Spain

Anji Bridge, Zhaoxian, China

Arkadiko Bridge, Arkadiko, Greece

B Bosphorus Bridge, Istanbul, Turkey

Bridge of Sighs, Venice, Italy

Bridge of the Slovak National Uprising, Bratislava, Slovakia

Brooklyn Bridge, New York, USA

C Charles Bridge, Prague, Czech Republic

D Danyang-Kunshan Grand Bridge, Jiangsu Province, China

Devil's Bridge, Kromlau, Germany

Duge Bridge, Xuanwwei, China

E Edmund Pettus Bridge, Selma, USA

Eshima Ohashi Bridge, Matsue, Japan

F Falkirk Wheel, Falkirk, Scotland

Forth Bridge, Edinburgh, Scotland

G Ganter Bridge, Brig, Switzerland

Garabit Viaduct, Ruynes-en-Margeride, France

George Washington Bridge, New York, USA

Golden Gate Bridge, San Francisco, USA

Göltzschtalbrücke, Reichenbach im Vogtland, Germany

H Harbour Bridge, Sydney, Australia

Hartland Bridge, Hartland, Canada

High Line Park, New York, USA

Howrah Bridge, Kolkata, India

Hussaini Bridge, Hussaini, Pakistan

I Iron Bridge, Telford, United Kingdom

K Kapellbrücke, Lucerne, Switzerland

L Lake Maracaibo Bridge, Venezuela

Lotus Bridge, Macau, China

Lyric Opera Bridge, Chicago, USA

M Manhattan Bridge, New York, USA

Menai Suspension Bridge, Bangor, United Kingdom

Millau Viaduct, Millau, France

Millennium Bridge, Gateshead, United Kingdom

Millennium Bridge, London, United Kingdom

Milvian Bridge, Rome, Italy

Moses Bridge, Halsteren, Netherlands

N Niagara Bridge, Niagara Falls, USA

Ø Øresund Bridge, Copenhagen-Malmö, Denmark-Sweden

P Pegasus Bridge, Bénouville, France

Plougastel Bridge, Brest, France

Pont Alexander III, Paris, France

Pont du Gard, Nîmes, France

Pont Jacques Chaban-Delmas, Bordeaux, France

Pont Neuf, Paris, France

Pont Saint-Bénézét, Avignon, France

Ponte Vecchio, Florence, Italy

Puente de la Mujer, Buenos Aires, Argentina

Q Quebec Bridge, Lévis, Canada

Queen Maxima Bridge, Amsterdam, Netherlands

Queshuachaca Bridge, Huinchiri, Peru

R Rialto Bridge, Venice, Italy

Rolling Bridge, London, United Kingdom

S Si-o-se-Pol Bridge, Isfahan, Iran

Stari Most, Mostar, Bosnia and Herzegovina

Stirling Bridge, Stirling, Scotland

Sunshine Skyway Bridge, St. Petersburg, USA

Széchenyi Chain Bridge, Budapest, Hungary

T Tacoma Narrows Bridge, Tacoma, USA

Tarr Steps, Withypool, United Kingdom

Textile Concrete Bridge, Albstadt, Germany

Tower Bridge, London, United Kingdom

Triple Bridge, Ljubljana, Slovenia

Twist Bridge, Jevnaker, Norway

U U Bein Bridge, Amarapura, Myanmar

Union Bridge, Berwick-upon-Tweed, United Kingdom

V Verrazzano-Narrows Bridge, New York, USA

W Wind and Rain Bridge, Chengyang, China

SOME MORE:

A Ada Bridge, Belgrade, Serbia

Aqueduct of Segovia, Segovia, Spain

B Bixby Creek Bridge, California, USA

H Hörn Bridge, Kiel, Germany

J Juscelino Kubitschek Bridge, Brasilia, Brazil

K Kakum Canopy Walk, Ghana, Africa

Karamagara Bridge, Turkey

Kintai Bridge, Iwakuni, Japan

L Lake Pontchartrain Causeway, Louisiana, USA

P Ponte Sant'Angelo, Rome, Italy

Puente Nuevo, Ronda, Spain

R Royal Gorge Bridge, Cañon City, USA

V Vasco da Gama Bridge, Lisbon, Portugal

Victoria Falls Bridge, Zimbabwe

AND THOSE
WHICH YOU HAVE DISCOVERED: